THE CAPTAIN
LESSONS ON CHRISTIAN PURPOSE

THE NAMES OF CHRIST ILLUSTRATRED

ACTIVITY BOOK

I0486832

THE NOC ILLUSTRATED ACTIVITY BOOKS: AN AMAZING WAY TO TEACH YOUTH THE MANY DIFFERENT CHARACTERS OF CHRIST FOUND IN THE HOLY SCRIPTURES.

ISBN: 1-441-46175-2

PRINTED IN THE UNITED STATES OF AMERICA

COVER PAGE DESIGNED BY DYNAMIC ANIMATION PRODUCTIONS, LLC

PREFACE

"For it became him, for whom are all things, and by whom are all things, in bringing many sons unto glory, to make the captain of their salvation perfect through sufferings." Hebrews 2:10 (KJV)

To our parents, teachers and guardians: it is a privilege to study God's word with your children and a blessing to train and discipline them for service in the master's cause. Along with their bibles, we strongly encourage your participation in the child's usage of this activity book.

SEE HOW MANY WORDS
YOU CAN CREATE OUT OF

CHARITY

"Charity suffereth long, and is kind; charity envieth not; charity vaunteth not itself, is not puffed up." ~ 1 Corinthians 13:4

_____

_____

_____

_____   _____

_____   _____

_____   _____

_____   _____

SECRET MESSAGE 1

A	B	C	D	E	F	G	H	I	J	K	L	M	N	O	P	Q	R	S	T	U	V	W	X	Y	Z
17	6	20	2	21	24	13	4	14	8	22	1	26	7	18	25	9	3	15	23	5	16	10	19	11	12

USE THE ABOVE KEYS TO DECODE THE MESSAGE BELOW

 B U T   G O   Y E   A N D
 6 5 23 13 18 11 21 17 7 2

 L E A R N   W H A T   T H A T
 1 21 17 3 7   10 4 17 23   23 4 17 23

 M E A N E T H ,   I   W I L L
 26 21 17 7 21 23 4   14   10 14 1 1

 H A V E   M E R C Y ,   A N D
 4 17 16 21   26 21 3 20 11   17 7 2

 N O T   S A C R I F I C E :
 7 18 23   15 17 20 3 14 24 14 20 21

 F O R   I   A M   N O T   C O M E
 24 18 3   14   17 26   7 18 23   20 18 26 21

 T O   C A L L   T H E
 23 18   20 17 1 1   23 4 21

 R I G H T E O U S ,   B U T
 3 14 13 4 23 21 18 5 15   6 5 23

 S I N N E R S   T O
 15 14 7 7 21 3 15   23 18

 R E P E N T A N C E .
 3 21 25 21 7 23 17 7 20 21

WHERE IS THIS TEXT FOUND?_____

FILL IN THE BLANK
COMMIT THESE VERSES OF SCRIPTURE TO MEMORY

AND HE SAID, _____. AND WHEN PETER WAS _____ DOWN OUT OF THE _____, HE _____ ON THE _____, TO GO TO JESUS. ~ MATTHEW 14:29

AND HE _____ UNTO THEM, YE SHALL _____ INDEED OF MY _____, AND BE _____ WITH THE BAPTISM THAT I AM _____ WITH: BUT TO SIT ON MY _____ HAND, AND ON MY _____, IS NOT MINE TO _____, BUT IT SHALL BE _____ TO THEM FOR WHOM IT IS _____ OF MY FATHER. ~ MATTHEW 20:23

AND HE _____ UNTO THEM, TAKE _____ FOR YOUR _____, NEITHER _____, NOR _____, NEITHER _____, NEITHER _____; NEITHER HAVE TWO _____ APIECE. ~ LUKE 9:3

AND SAITH UNTO _____, GO YOUR WAY INTO THE _____ OVER _____ YOU: AND AS SOON AS YE BE _____ INTO IT, YE SHALL _____ A _____ TIED, WHEREON NEVER MAN _____; _____ HIM, AND _____ HIM. ~ MARK 11:2

THAT YE MAY _____ AND _____ AT MY TABLE IN MY _____, AND SIT ON _____ JUDGING THE _____ TRIBES OF _____. ~ LUKE 22:30

BUT GO _____ TO THE LOST _____ OF THE _____ OF _____. ~ MATTHEW 10:6

AND JUDAS ALSO, WHICH _____ HIM, _____ THE _____: FOR JESUS _____ _____ _____ WITH HIS _____. ~ JOHN 18:2

NOW AS HE _____ BY THE SEA OF _____, HE SAW _____ AND _____ HIS BROTHER _____ A _____ INTO THE _____: FOR THEY WERE _____. ~ MARK 1:16

THEN WERE THERE _____ UNTO HIM LITTLE _____, THAT HE _____ PUT HIS _____ ON THEM, AND _____: AND THE DISCIPLES _____ THEM. ~ MATTHEW 19:13

AND HE _____ UNTO THEM, BUT _____ SAY YE _____ I AM? AND _____ ANSWERETH AND SAITH UNTO HIM, _____ ART THE _____. ~ MARK 8:29

MATCH THESE WORDS TO SCRIPTURE
Scriptures are taken from the KJV Bible

REASON   EXODUS 5:14

POINT   EPHESIANS 4:29

MEANING   GENESIS 47:3

OCCUPATION   LUKE 5:22

TASK   JAMES 2:10

GATHERING   JOHN 11:15

INTENT   DANIEL 8:15

STANDARD   MATTHEW 25:24

CHRISTIAN PURPOSE SIMPLIFIED
Crossword Puzzle 1

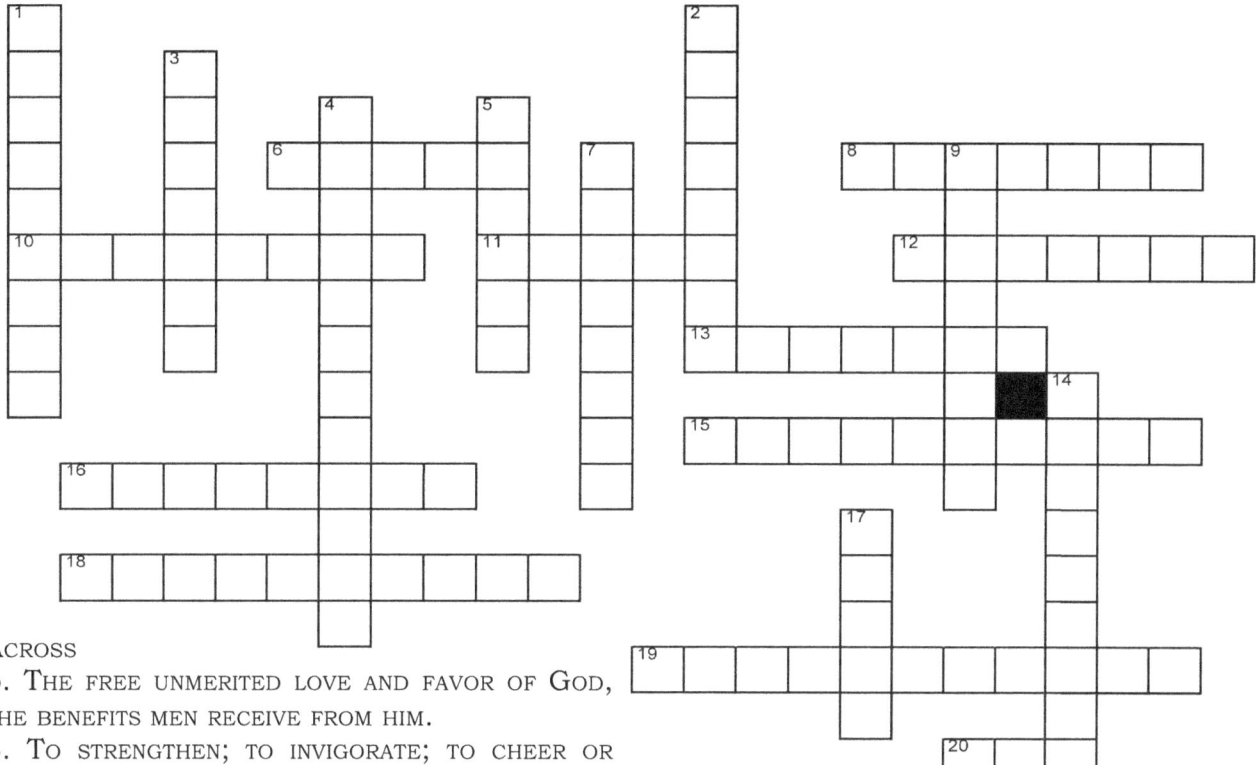

Across

6. The free unmerited love and favor of God, the benefits men receive from him.

8. To strengthen; to invigorate; to cheer or enliven. To strengthen the mind when depressed or enfeebled; to console.

10. Lowly; modest; meek; submissive; not proud or haughty. Having a deep sense of unworthiness in the sight of God.

11. In a general sense, a state of quiet or tranquility; freedom from disturbance or agitation.

12. The act of repairing, as a breach; to supply a part broken or defective. To correct; to set right.

13. Partaking; having a part with another; enjoying or suffering with others.

15. Testifying; telling of a fact or event. That which furnishes evidence or proof.

16. Suffering affliction, pain, toil, calamity, with a calm, unruffled temper; endurance without murmuring.

18. Suffering with another; painful sympathy; a sorrow excited by the distress or misfortunes of another; pity.

19. To attend and serve; to perform service in any office, sacred or secular. To take care of the wants and needs of others.

20. The passion or emotion excited by the acquisition or expectation of good; rejoice.

Down

1. To speak on the gospel way of salvation and urge to repentance and acceptance of the terms of salvation.

2. Good will; benevolence; delighting in contributing to the happiness of others.

3. To think favorably of their fellow men, and to do them good.

4. Full conformity to fact or reality; in exact accordance with. Honesty.

5. One that aids or assists; an assistant; one that furnishes or administers a remedy.

7. The act of instructing; informing; to communicate to another the knowledge of that of which he was before ignorant.

9. Mildness of temper; softness; gentleness; not easily provoked or irritated; yielding.

14. Pure; unmixed, unhurt; uninjured; not assumed or said for the sake of appearance.

17. To place confidence in; a reliance of the mind on the integrity of friendship or other sound principle of another person.

Crossword Puzzle 1: Answers found on page 37

5

JOURNAL OF PURPOSE

CHARITY: In a more particular sense, love, kindness, affection, tenderness, springing from natural relations; as the charities of father, son and brother.

Find as many "immediate family members" to do a kind deed for by giving.
For each week, note what you have done in the appropriate box of this journal.

WEEK 1	WEEK 2	WEEK 3	WEEK 4
DAY 1			
DAY 2			
DAY 3			
DAY 4			
DAY 5			
DAY 6			

"Charity suffereth long, and is kind; charity envieth not; charity vaunteth not itself, is not puffed up." ~ 1 Corinthians 13:4

PURPOSE IS KEY

SEEK AND FIND YOUR WAY THROUGH THE MAZE BELOW

START

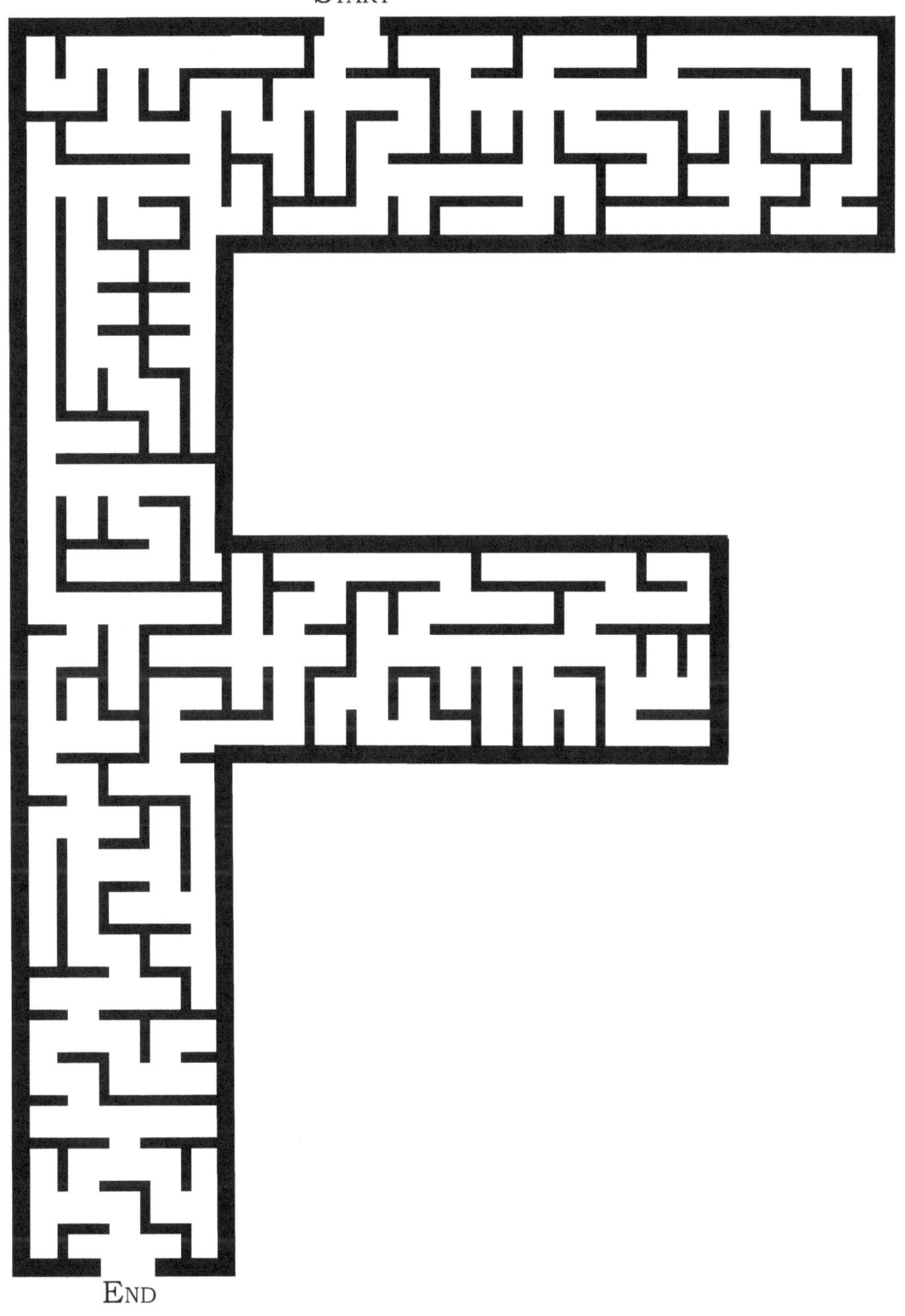

END

COLORING ACTIVITY

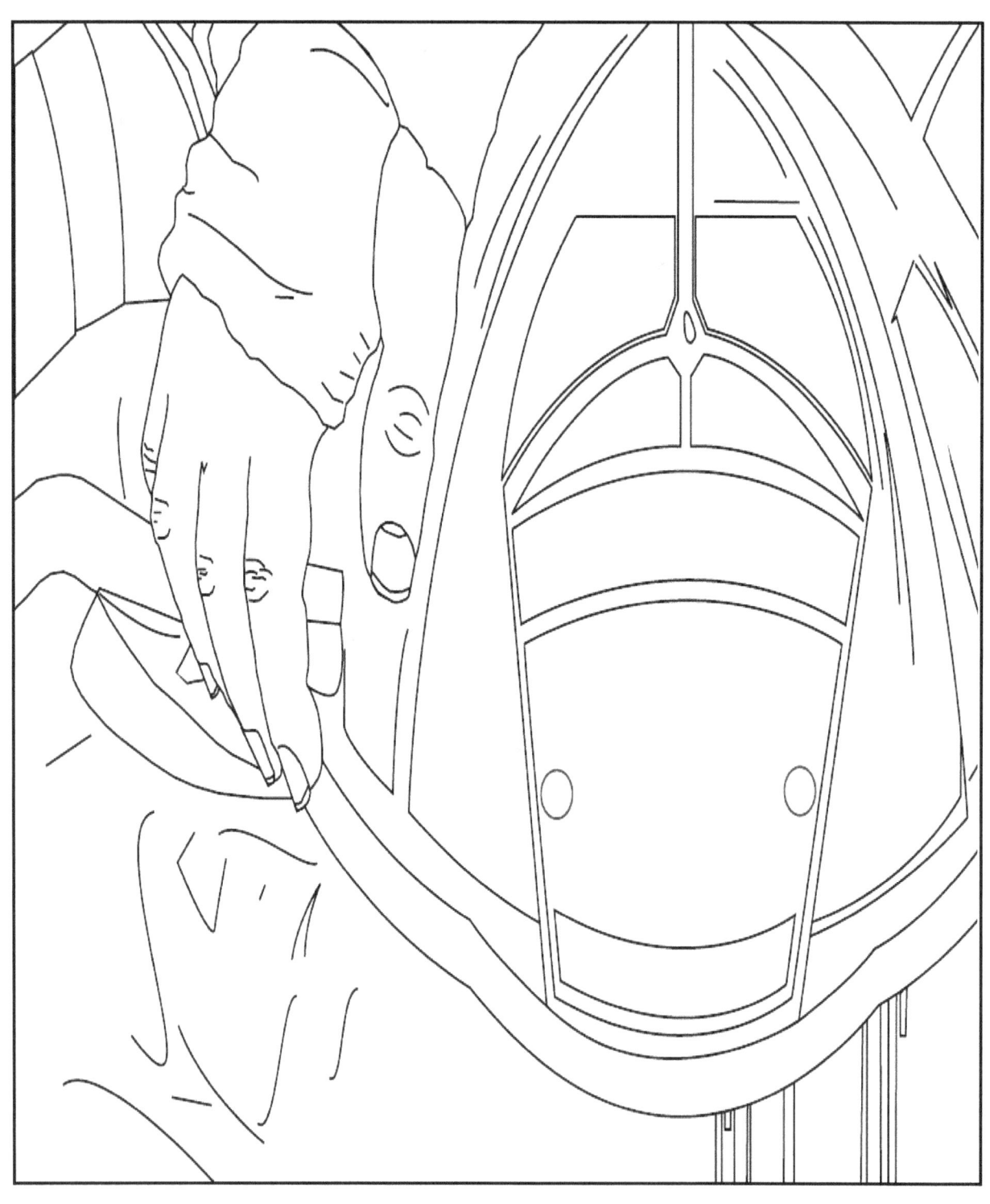

THE CAPTAIN

BIBLE TRIVIA 1: MISSION OF THE 12

1. What were Peter and Andrew's occupation?

A) Market traders   B) Tax collectors   C) Fishermen   D) Carpenters

2. What group of people did Jesus send His disciples out to teach first?

A) Gentiles   B) Samaritans   C) Philistines   D) House of Israel

3. Which of the following items were they allowed to take?

A) Money   B) Two coats   C) Shoes   D) None of these

4. Which disciple tried to walk on water as Jesus was doing?

A) James   B) Peter   C) John   D) Philip

5. When Jesus asked "whom say ye that I am?", what was Peter's reply?

A) Thou art the Christ   B) Thou art Elijah   C) Thou art a Moses   D) Thou art John the Baptist

6. What did the disciples do when the people brought their children to Christ?

A) They welcomed them   B) They gave them food   C) They rebuked them   D) They baptized them

7. Before entering Jerusalem for the last time, Jesus sent two disciples to bring what?

A) colt   B) fruit   C) glass of water   D) young lamb

8. Which one of the disciples betrayed Jesus?

A) Andrew   B) Bartholomew   C) Judas Iscariot   D) Thomas

Bible Trivia 1: Answers found on page 35

UNSCRAMBLE THE WORDS BELOW

EPTRNEEANC   _____

DCBNOEIEE   _____

BISMONIUSS   _____

FTSONMARR   _____

OSRREET   _____

RITYOVC   _____

STANGIF   _____

CAPEE   _____

FOOTMCR   _____

TRIMENSI   _____

UNSCRAMBLE EXERCISE 1: ANSWERS FOUND ON PAGE 36

CHRISTIAN PURPOSE SIMPLIFIED

FIND THESE WORDS IN THE FOREST OF LETTERS

```
C H M A J N I P P H U M I L I T Y C S F T O H T S
T U J G C O M F O R T D S A X T W T V D Q F P Q I
O R G O Q Y E I E L F U D S Q L V O O Y E A G U N
J J U E Y R G Z K Q E U A R D J G Q G C S B J X C
Z A O T I O N I H M Q Q F O K S P N N V W X Q G E
M D G C H E O J T E P G E W F H I E X H I L C L R
E P H M J F N A C C S T O N G H I G W P T O P P I
N H R I B S U A V S V L Y N C T E M K H N H Y N T
D T E E C P L L E H I K I A A I Y V U R E E O B Y
I U R L A R Q N N N A R E P D T W F X F S I H T S
N G T U P C K S I E E T Q B I I R W T L S Z Y T H
G P U L S E H P L T S P G R W C B W W S I K N O A
E U L J E T R I S G I S A R F B F R A D N L L X R
M S N M V R K I N F G H V C A T Z P Y G G Q U M I
J A V G T V N U Q G C F P U C C M M Y R R I W J N
V E Y C K I P O A C W W V R N O E K S A K Y O I G
B X K P M K K I N D N E S S C N P E A C E B X D D
```

JOY	PEACE	KINDNESS
HELPER	CHARITY	COMFORT
TRUST	SHARING	GRACE
TRUTHFULNESS	COMPASSION	PATIENCE
MEEKNESS	WITNESSING	HUMILITY
SINCERITY	MENDING	MINISTERING
TEACHING	PREACHING	

WORD SEARCH 1: ANSWERS FOUND ON PAGE 37

SEE HOW MANY WORDS
YOU CAN CREATE OUT OF
TEACHING

"I WAS DAILY WITH YOU IN THE TEMPLE TEACHING, AND YE TOOK ME NOT:
BUT THE SCRIPTURES MUST BE FULFILLED." ~ MARK 14:49

_____

_____

_____

_____   _____

_____   _____

_____   _____

_____   _____

SECRET MESSAGE 2

A	B	C	D	E	F	G	H	I	J	K	L	M	N	O	P	Q	R	S	T	U	V	W	X	Y	Z
12	22	4	17	3	14	24	16	5	18	1	11	2	21	6	10	20	7	26	13	25	8	15	23	9	19

USE THE ABOVE KEYS TO DECODE THE MESSAGE BELOW

A N D   L E T   U S   N O T
12 21 17   11 3 13   25 26   21 6 13

B E   W E A R Y   I N   W E L L
22 3   15 3 12 7 9   5 21   15 3 11 11

D O I N G :   F O R   I N   D U E
17 6 5 21 24   14 6 7   5 21   17 25 3

S E A S O N   W E   S H A L L
26 3 12 26 6 21   15 3   26 16 12 11 11

R E A P ,   I F   W E   F A I N T
7 3 12 10   5 14   15 3   14 12 5 21 13

N O T .
21 6 13

WHERE IS THIS TEXT FOUND? _____

SECRET MESSAGE 2: ANSWERS FOUND ON PAGE 35

JOURNAL OF PURPOSE

INTERCESSION: The act of interceding; mediation; interposition between parties at variance, with a view of reconciliation; prayer or solicitation to one party in favor of another, sometimes against another.

Find as many "immediate family members" to pray for or intercede on their behalf. For each week, insert what you have done in the appropriate box of this journal.

	WEEK 1	WEEK 2	WEEK 3	WEEK 4
DAY 1				
DAY 2				
DAY 3				
DAY 4				
DAY 5				
DAY 6				

"God hath not cast away his people which he foreknew. Wot ye not what the scripture saith of Elias? how he maketh intercession to God against Israel." ~ Romans 11:2

14

MATCH THESE WORDS TO SCRIPTURE
SCRIPTURES ARE TAKEN FROM THE KJV BIBLE

BELIEF   1 CORINTHIANS 15:24

STANDARD   HEBREWS 4:14

OPINION   GENESIS 46:34

RULE   LUKE 19:13

LAW   JEREMIAH 51:27

TRADE   2 THESSALONIANS 2:13

PROFESSION   EXODUS 12:49

OCCUPY   JOB 32:10

MATCHING EXERCISE 2: ANSWERS FOUND ON PAGE 36

CHRISTIAN PURPOSE

FIND THESE WORDS IN THE FOREST OF LETTERS

```
T D P K S R M X O V H D E L I V E R I N G D I J F
H F C V R V R U B I G B Z X I A Y Y J R Y P Z P G
Q N L H E P J H E C O S J K X U Y D C P F V M N C
U G M J P D W F Y T B F S L I S D Z A G M E I S Y
N M D T E F T F I O T H W U M T N Z N A D Y U U G
I Y P Z N A V K N R R N I U R A O I Q T A K J B X
F W U S T S R C G I A K H N S R W S M R Y W H M P
Y P C S I T O Q D O N C C V T E E L P W N X R I F
I R J E N I Q Z T U S R T X N E Z N I H L Q S T L
N O H R G N D Y X S F A E E J Y R W D D U T Y T A
G V V V K G Q W I F O E R S T R X C E E Z X T I B
T I E I Z E Q R Z R V C E T W Y M E V R W W N O
M N G N O V E R C O M I N G L O L M R D T I J G R
X G J G H G R T P H I A U E U Q R P P K I K N L I
D W G S W Q L G M P N R S W J L H I W K L N C G N
X S N U T O P T J S G I J A M Z A W N K C H G L G
B Z K G N F O R G I V I N G B G L Q V G E F Y W H
```

REPENTING	FORGIVING	OBEYING	SURRENDERING
SUBMITTING	SERVING	DUTY	INTERCEDING
TRANSFORMING	RENEWING	PROVING	RESTORING
UNIFYING	OVERCOMING	VICTORIOUS	DELIVERING
LABORING	PRAYING	FASTING	

WORD SEARCH 2: ANSWERS FOUND ON PAGE 37

FILL IN THE BLANK
COMMIT THESE VERSES OF SCRIPTURE TO MEMORY

THERE IS A _____ HERE, WHICH HATH FIVE _____ LOAVES, AND TWO SMALL _____: BUT WHAT ARE THEY _____ SO MANY? ~ JOHN 6:9 (ALSO SEE VERSE 8)

JESUS _____, HE IT IS, TO _____ I SHALL GIVE A _____, WHEN I HAVE _____ IT. AND WHEN HE HAD _____ THE SOP, HE GAVE IT TO _____ _____, THE SON OF SIMON. ~ JOHN 13:26

AND HE THAT _____ HIM HAD _____ THEM A _____, SAYING, WHOMSOEVER I SHALL _____, THAT _____ IS HE; _____ HIM, AND _____ HIM AWAY _____. ~ MARK 14:44

AFTER _____ THINGS JESUS _____ HIMSELF AGAIN TO THE _____ AT THE SEA OF _____; AND ON THIS _____ SHOWED HE HIMSELF. ~ JOHN 21:1 (ALSO SEE VERSE 13)

AND AFTER _____ DAYS JESUS _____ WITH HIM PETER, AND JAMES, AND JOHN, AND _____ THEM UP INTO AN HIGH _____ APART BY _____: AND HE WAS _____ BEFORE THEM. ~ MARK 9:2

SIMON PETER SAITH UNTO HIM, _____, NOT MY _____ ONLY, BUT ALSO MY _____ AND MY _____. ~ JOHN 13:9

THEN SAITH HE TO _____, REACH _____ THY _____, AND BEHOLD MY _____; AND _____ HITHER THY HAND, AND _____ IT INTO MY _____: AND BE NOT _____, BUT _____. ~ JOHN 20:27

WHOSOEVER _____ SHALL _____ HIMSELF AS THIS _____ CHILD, THE _____ IS _____ IN THE_____ OF HEAVEN. ~ MATTHEW 18:4

_____ SAITH UNTO HIM, LORD, _____ US THE _____, AND IT _____ US. ~ JOHN 14:8

AND WHEN HIS _____ JAMES AND JOHN SAW THIS, THEY SAID, LORD, WILT _____ THAT WE _____ FIRE TO _____ DOWN FROM _____, AND _____ THEM, EVEN AS _____ DID? ~ LUKE 9:54

17

CHRISTIAN PURPORSE
CROSSWORD PUZZLE 2

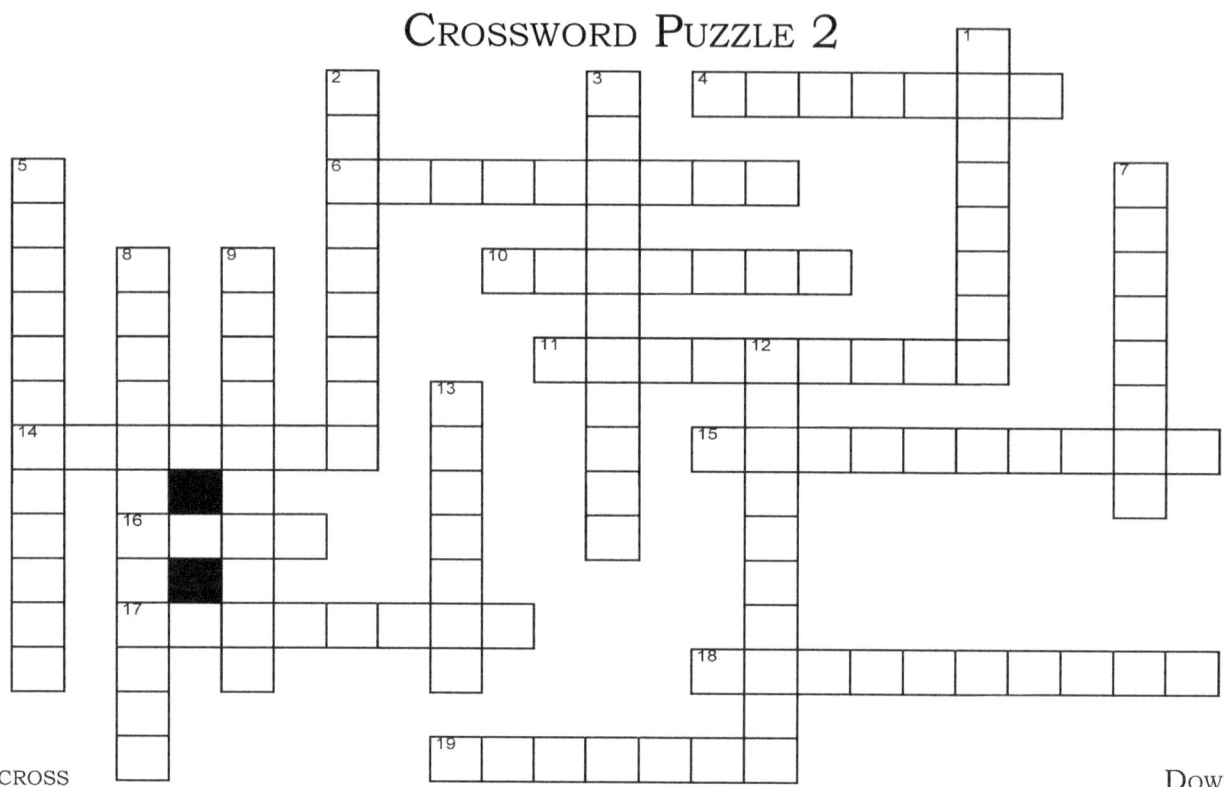

ACROSS

4. SOLEMN ADDRESSES OF ADORATION, SUPPLICATION FOR MERCY AND FORGIVENESS, OR AN EXPRESSION OF GRATITUDE TO GOD. TALKING TO GOD.

6. THE ACT OF FEELING SORRY FOR ANY THING DONE OR SAID; SORROW OR DEEP CONTRITION FOR SIN.

10. LABORING OF BODY AND MIND, PERFORMED AT THE COMMAND OF A SUPERIOR, OR THE PURSUANCE OF DUTY, OR FOR THE BENEFIT OF ANOTHER.

11. REPLACING; TO RETURN; AS A PERSON OR THING TO A FORMER PLACE. TO BRING BACK.

14. THE ACT OF FOLLOWING A COMMAND; WHAT IS REQUIRED OR FORBIDDEN BY AUTHORITY.

15. RELEASING FROM CAPTIVITY, SLAVERY, OPPRESSION, OR ANY RESTRAINT.

16. THAT WHICH A PERSON OWES TO ANOTHER; THAT WHICH A PERSON IS BOUND, BY ANY NATURAL, MORAL OR LEGAL OBLIGATION.

17. MAKING NEW AGAIN; REPAIRING; RE-ESTABLISHING; REPEATING; REVIVING; RENOVATING.

18. THE ADVANTAGE OR SUPERIORITY GAINED OVER ENEMIES, OVER PASSIONS AND APPETITES, OR OVER TEMPTATIONS, OR ANY COMPETITION.

19. THE ACT OF ABSTAINING FROM FOOD.

DOWN

1. THE ACT OF MAKING ONENESS BETWEEN 2 OR MORE ITEMS OR PEOPLE; AGREEING.

2. THE PARDON OF AN OFFENDER; THE PARDON OR REMISSION OF AN OFFENSE OR CRIME.

3. THE ACT OF MEDIATION; INTERPOSITION BETWEEN PARTIES AT VARIANCE, WITH A VIEW TO RECONCILIATION. TO COME BETWEEN PARTIES IN CONFLICT.

5. THE ACT OF CHANGING THE SHAPE OR APPEARANCE; TO CHANGE THE NATURAL DISPOSITION AND TEMPER OF MAN.

7. EXERTING OF MUSCULAR STRENGTH, OR BODILY EXERTION WHICH OCCASIONS WEARINESS; INTELLECTUAL EXERTION.

8. THE ACT OF YIELDING TO THE POWER OF ANOTHER; TO GIVE OR DELIVER UP POSSESSION UPON COMPULSION OR DEMAND. TO GIVE UP.

9. THE ACT OF ACKNOWLEDGING INFERIORITY OR DEPENDENCE; HUMBLING; SURRENDER.

12. THE ACT OF CONQUERING; TO VANQUISH; TO SUBDUE; TO SURMOUNT; BE VICTORIOUS.

13. TO ASCERTAIN SOME UNKNOWN QUALITY OR TRUTH BY AN EXPERIMENT, OR BY A TEST.

CROSSWORD PUZZLE 2: ANSWERS FOUND ON PAGE 37

PURPOSE IS KEY

SEEK AND FIND YOUR WAY THROUGH THE MAZE BELOW

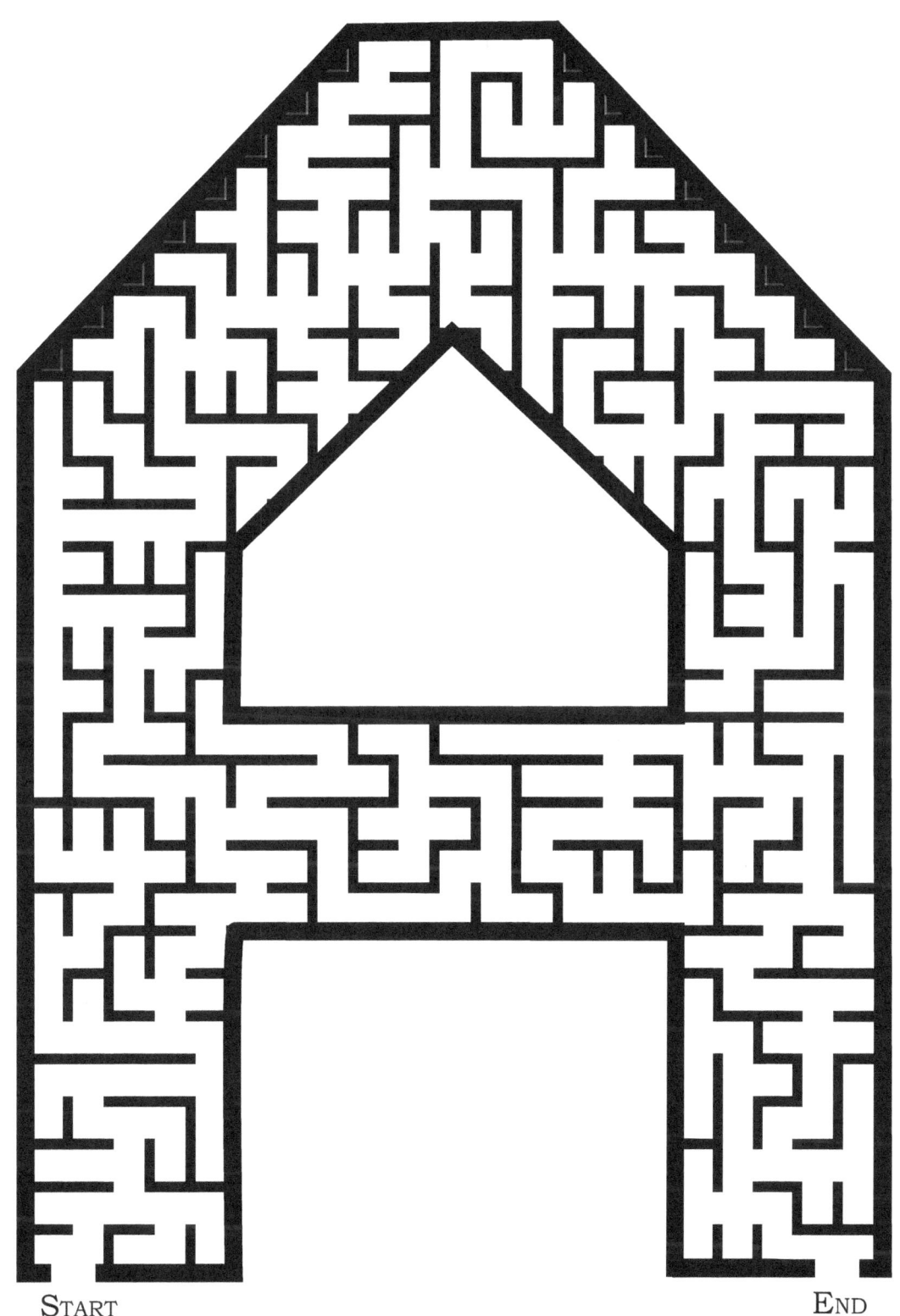

START

END

SECRET MESSAGE 3

A	B	C	D	E	F	G	H	I	J	K	L	M	N	O	P	Q	R	S	T	U	V	W	X	Y	Z
22	16	10	4	1	8	13	20	25	14	2	12	19	26	11	3	15	21	24	9	5	23	7	17	6	18

USE THE ABOVE KEYS TO DECODE THE MESSAGE BELOW

$\overline{16}\ \overline{21}\ \overline{1}\ \overline{9}\ \overline{20}\ \overline{21}\ \overline{1}\ \overline{26}$, $\overline{25}\ \overline{8}$ $\overline{22}$

$\overline{19}\ \overline{22}\ \overline{26}$ $\overline{16}\ \overline{1}$ $\overline{11}\ \overline{23}\ \overline{1}\ \overline{21}\ \overline{9}\ \overline{22}\ \overline{2}\ \overline{1}\ \overline{26}$

$\overline{25}\ \overline{26}$ $\overline{22}$ $\overline{8}\ \overline{22}\ \overline{5}\ \overline{12}\ \overline{9}$, $\overline{6}\ \overline{1}$

$\overline{7}\ \overline{20}\ \overline{25}\ \overline{10}\ \overline{20}$ $\overline{22}\ \overline{21}\ \overline{1}$ $\overline{24}\ \overline{3}\ \overline{25}\ \overline{21}\ \overline{25}\ \overline{9}\ \overline{5}\ \overline{22}\ \overline{12}$,

$\overline{21}\ \overline{1}\ \overline{24}\ \overline{9}\ \overline{11}\ \overline{21}\ \overline{1}$ $\overline{24}\ \overline{5}\ \overline{10}\ \overline{20}$ $\overline{22}\ \overline{26}$

$\overline{11}\ \overline{26}\ \overline{1}$ $\overline{25}\ \overline{26}$ $\overline{9}\ \overline{20}\ \overline{1}$ $\overline{24}\ \overline{3}\ \overline{25}\ \overline{21}\ \overline{25}\ \overline{9}$

$\overline{11}\ \overline{8}$ $\overline{19}\ \overline{1}\ \overline{1}\ \overline{2}\ \overline{26}\ \overline{1}\ \overline{24}\ \overline{24}$;

$\overline{10}\ \overline{11}\ \overline{26}\ \overline{24}\ \overline{25}\ \overline{4}\ \overline{1}\ \overline{21}\ \overline{25}\ \overline{26}\ \overline{13}$ $\overline{9}\ \overline{20}\ \overline{6}\ \overline{24}\ \overline{1}\ \overline{12}\ \overline{8}$,

$\overline{12}\ \overline{1}\ \overline{24}\ \overline{9}$ $\overline{9}\ \overline{20}\ \overline{11}\ \overline{5}$ $\overline{22}\ \overline{12}\ \overline{24}\ \overline{11}$ $\overline{16}\ \overline{1}$

$\overline{9}\ \overline{1}\ \overline{19}\ \overline{3}\ \overline{9}\ \overline{1}\ \overline{4}$.

WHERE IS THIS TEXT FOUND? _____

SEE HOW MANY WORDS
YOU CAN CREATE OUT OF
SERVING

"SERVING THE LORD WITH ALL HUMILITY OF MIND, AND WITH MANY TEARS, AND TEMPTATIONS, WHICH BEFELL ME BY THE LYING IN WAIT OF THE JEWS."
~ ACTS 20:19

_____

_____

_____   _____

_____   _____

_____   _____

_____   _____

JOURNAL OF PURPOSE

HELPING: USEFULNESS; PROVIDING ASSISTANCE.

FIND AS MANY PEOPLE TO DO A KIND DEED FOR BY HELPING.
FOR EACH WEEK, INSERT WHAT YOU HAVE DONE IN THE APPROPRIATE BOX OF THIS JOURNAL.

	WEEK 1	WEEK 2	WEEK 3	WEEK 4
DAY 1				
DAY 2				
DAY 3				
DAY 4				
DAY 5				
DAY 6				

"THEN ROSE UP ZERUBBABEL THE SON OF SHEALTIEL, AND JESHUA THE SON OF JOZADAK, AND BEGAN TO BUILD THE HOUSE OF GOD WHICH IS AT JERUSALEM: AND WITH THEM WERE THE PROPHETS OF GOD HELPING THEM." ~ EZRA 5:2

SEE HOW MANY WORDS
YOU CAN CREATE OUT OF

INTERCESSION

"WHO IS HE THAT CONDEMNETH? IT IS CHRIST THAT DIED, YEA RATHER, THAT IS RISEN AGAIN,
WHO IS EVEN AT THE RIGHT HAND OF GOD, WHO ALSO MAKETH INTERCESSION FOR US."
~ ROMANS 8:34

_____

_____

_____

_____   _____

_____   _____

_____   _____

_____   _____

BIBLE TRIVIA 2: MISSION OF THE 12

1. WHAT SIGN DID THE BETRAYER GIVE THAT JESUS WAS THE MAN THE MOB WANTED?
A) HE GAVE HIM A   B) MONEY   C) A SLAP   D) A KISS
   LIGHTED TORCH

2. WHAT EVENT DID PETER, JAMES AND JOHN WITNESS ON THE MOUNTAIN WITH JESUS?
A) RESURRECTION   B) ASCENSION   C) TRANSFIGURATION D) ATONEMENT

3. THE BOY WITH THE 5 LOAVES AND 2 FISHES WAS BROUGHT TO JESUS BY WHICH DISCIPLE?
A) PETER   B) ANDREW   C) JAMES   D) JOHN

4. WHICH PARTS OF HIS BODY DID PETER ASK JESUS TO WASH AFTER BEING TOLD THAT UNLESS JESUS
   WASHED HIS FEET HE WOULD HAVE NO PART WITH HIM?
A) HEAD, FACE, EARS   B) FEET, HANDS, EARS   C) FEET, HANDS   D) FEET, HANDS,
                                                                        HEAD

5. WHAT DID JESUS GIVE TO JUDAS BEFORE HE LEFT TO BETRAY HIM?
A) THE MONEY BAG   B) A PIECE OF BREAD   C) A PIECE OF FISH D) A CUP OF WINE
                            DIPPED IN THE DISH

6. WHICH OF THE 12 DISCIPLES ASKED JESUS TO SHOW THEM THE FATHER?
A) PHILIP   B) BARTHOLOMEW   C) THOMAS   D) MATTHEW

7. WHAT DID THOMAS REQUEST TO SEE BEFORE HE WOULD BELIEVE THAT JESUS WAS RAISED FROM THE
   DEAD?
A) THE NAIL MARKS IN   B) JESUS APPEARING   C) THE HOLY SPIRIT D) JESUS' EMPTY
   JESUS' HANDS   BEFORE HIM   APPEARING   TOMB

8. AFTER HIS RESURRECTION, WHAT DID JESUS AND THE DISCIPLES HAVE FOR BREAKFAST BY THE SEA
   OF TIBERIAS?
A) CHEESES   B) BREAD   C) FISH   D) MEAT

BIBLE TRIVIA 2: ANSWERS FOUND ON PAGE 35

SECRET MESSAGE 4

A	B	C	D	E	F	G	H	I	J	K	L	M	N	O	P	Q	R	S	T	U	V	W	X	Y	Z
9	4	15	21	26	10	18	5	16	1	13	6	23	8	2	14	24	11	3	17	25	7	19	12	20	22

USE THE ABOVE KEYS TO DECODE THE MESSAGE BELOW

__ __   __ __ __   __ __   __ __ __ ,
20 26   9 11 26   2 10   18 2 21

__ __ __ __ __ __   __ __ __ __ __ __ __ __ ,
6 16 17 17 6 26   15 5 16 6 21 11 26 8

__ __ __   __ __ __ __   __ __ __ __ __ __ __ __
9 8 21   5 9 7 26   2 7 26 11 15 2 23 26

__ __ __ __ :   __ __ __ __ __ __ __
17 5 26 23   4 26 15 9 25 3 26

__ __ __ __ __ __ __   __ __   __ __   __ __ __ __
18 11 26 9 17 26 11   16 3   5 26   17 5 9 17

__ __   __ __   __ __ __ ,   __ __ __ __   __ __
16 3   16 8   20 2 25   17 5 9 8   5 26

__ __ __ __   __ __   __ __   __ __ __
17 5 9 17   16 3   16 8   17 5 26

__ __ __ __ __ .
19 2 11 6 21

WHERE IS THIS TEXT FOUND? _____

SECRET MESSAGE 4: ANSWERS FOUND ON PAGE 35

JOURNAL OF PURPOSE

SHARING: DISTRIBUTING, ALLOTING; TO LET SOMEONE USE OR ENJOY SOMETHING THAT IS YOURS

FIND AS MANY PEOPLE IN NEED TO DO A KIND DEED FOR BY SHARING.
FOR EACH WEEK, INSERT WHAT YOU HAVE DONE IN THE APPROPRIATE BOX OF THIS JOURNAL.

	WEEK 1	WEEK 2	WEEK 3	WEEK 4
DAY 1				
DAY 2				
DAY 3				
DAY 4				
DAY 5				
DAY 6				

"AND THE KING SHALL ANSWER AND SAY UNTO THEM, VERILY I SAY UNTO YOU, INASMUCH AS YE HAVE DONE IT UNTO ONE OF THE LEAST OF THESE MY BRETHREN, YE HAVE DONE IT UNTO ME." ~ MATTHEW 25:40

PURPOSE IS KEY

SEEK AND FIND YOUR WAY THROUGH THE MAZE BELOW

START

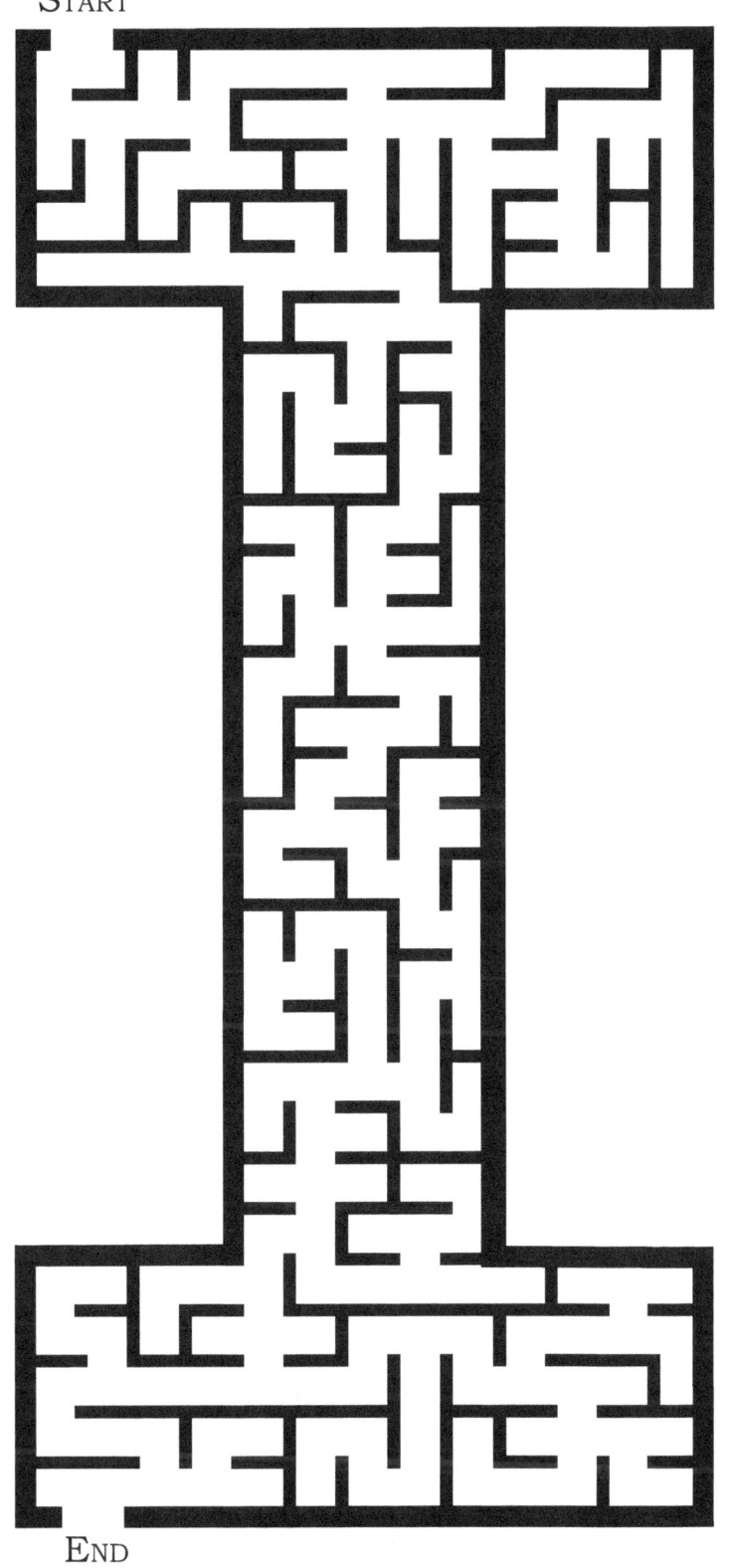

END

COLORING ACTIVITY

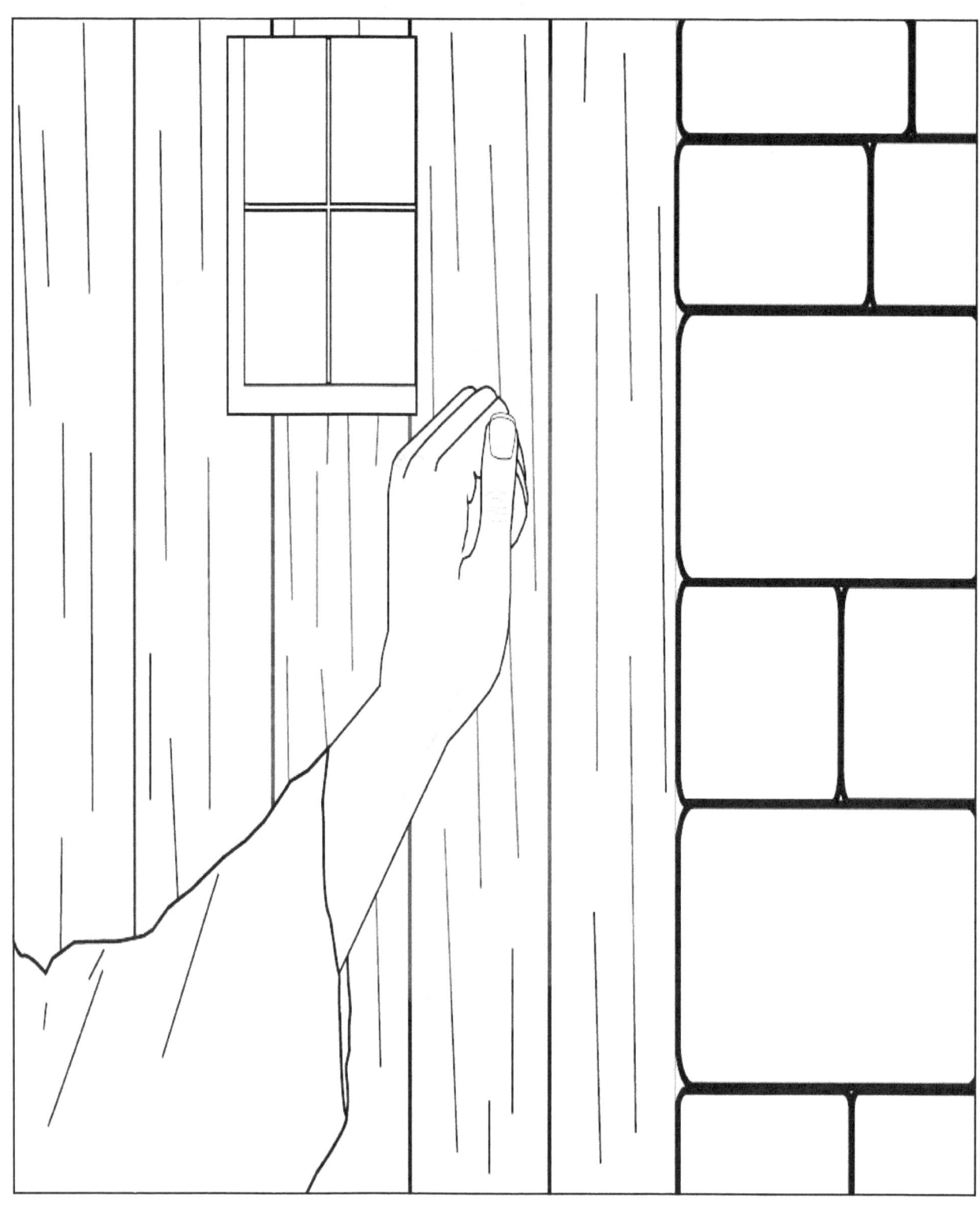

THE KNOCK

SEE HOW MANY WORDS
YOU CAN CREATE OUT OF

LONGSUFFERING

"But thou, O Lord, art a God full of compassion, and gracious, longsuffering, and plenteous in mercy and truth."
~ Psalm 86:15

_____

_____

_____

_____   _____

_____   _____

_____   _____

_____   _____

PURPOSE IS KEY

SEEK AND FIND YOUR WAY THROUGH THE MAZE BELOW

START

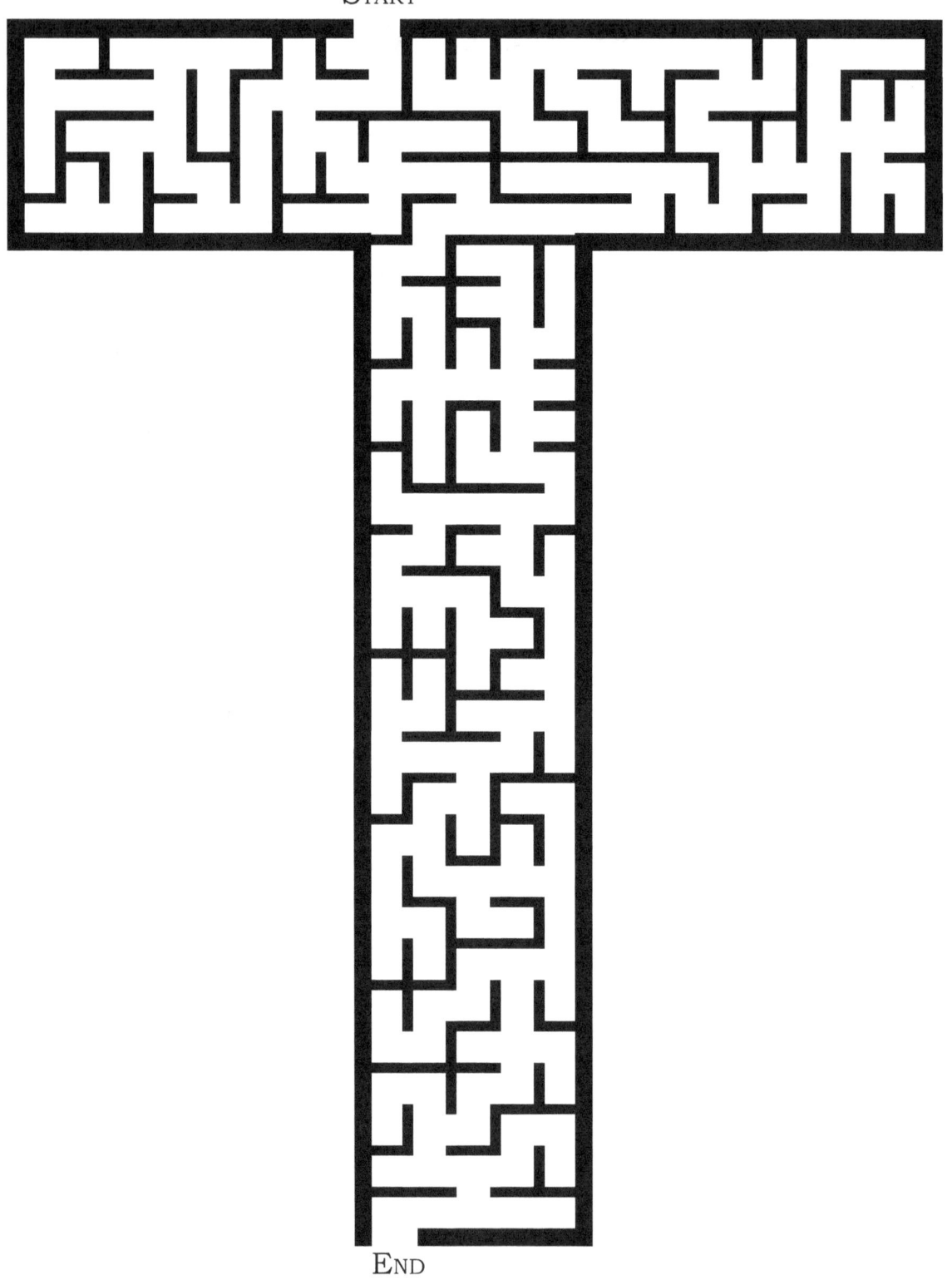

END

30

JOURNAL OF PURPOSE

EDIFY: To strengthen; to invigorate; to cheer or enliven. Light excelleth in comforting the spirits of men.

Find as many people to give words of encouragement to.
For each week, insert what you have done in the appropriate box of this journal.

	WEEK 1	WEEK 2	WEEK 3	WEEK 4
DAY 1				
DAY 2				
DAY 3				
DAY 4				
DAY 5				
DAY 6				

"Therefore comfort yourselves together, and edify one another, even as also ye do."
~ 1 Thessalonians 5:11

31

PURPOSE IS KEY

SEEK AND FIND YOUR WAY THROUGH THE MAZE BELOW

START

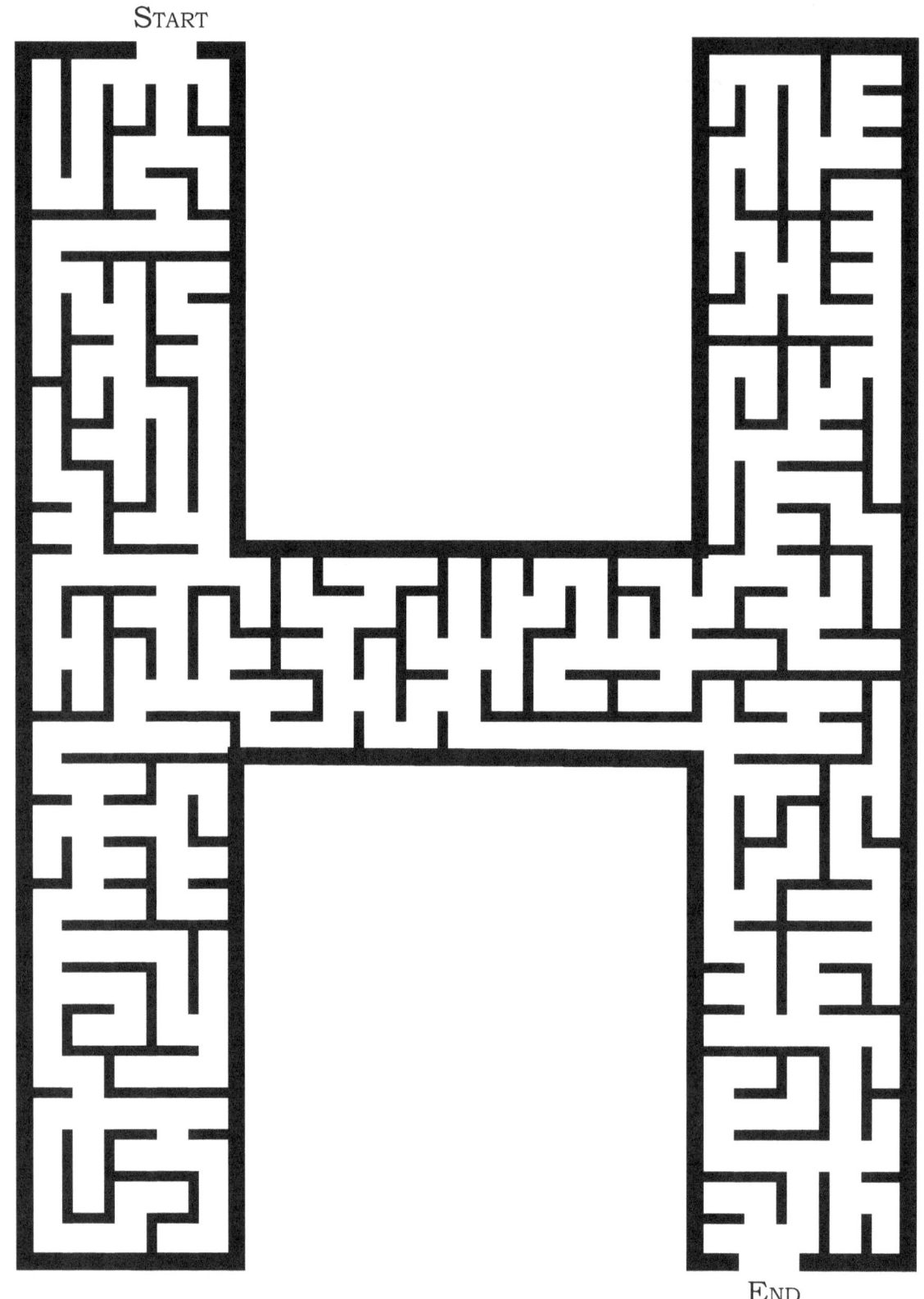

END

UNSCRAMBLE THESE WORDS

EFEGSOVNRSI   _____

SRDURNERE   _____

ICTSNORINSEE   _____

WEGRINEN   _____

VOMEROCE   _____

DANCERIVEEL   _____

GELNOWLID   _____

PEELRH   _____

SCENERY   _____

HEAPCR   _____

UNSCRAMBLE EXERCISE 2: ANSWERS FOUND ON PAGE 36

SEE HOW MANY WORDS
YOU CAN CREATE OUT OF
SHARING

"BENJAMIN SHALL RAVIN AS A WOLF: IN THE MORNING HE SHALL DEVOUR THE PREY,
AND AT NIGHT HE SHALL DIVIDE THE SPOIL."
~ GENESIS 49:27

_____

_____

_____   _____

_____   _____

_____   _____

_____   _____

ANSWER PAGES

SECRET MESSAGE 1

BUT GO YE AND LEARN WHAT THAT MEANETH, I WILL HAVE MERCY, AND NOT SACRIFICE: FOR I AM NOT COME TO CALL THE RIGHTEOUS, BUT SINNERS TO REPENTANCE.

MATTHEW 9:13

SECRET MESSAGE 2

AND LET US NOT BE WEARY IN WELL DOING: FOR IN DUE SEASON WE SHALL REAP, IF WE FAINT NOT.

GALATIANS 6:9

SECRET MESSAGE 3

BRETHREN, IF A MAN BE OVERTAKEN IN A FAULT, YE WHICH ARE SPIRITUAL, RESTORE SUCH AN ONE IN THE SPIRIT OF MEEKNESS; CONSIDERING THYSELF, LEST THOU ALSO BE TEMPTED.

GALATIANS 6:1

SECRET MESSAGE 4

YE ARE OF GOD, LITTLE CHILDREN, AND HAVE OVERCOME THEM: BECAUSE GREATER IS HE THAT IS IN YOU, THAN HE THAT IS IN THE WORLD.

1 JOHN 4:4

BIBLE TRIVIA 1:
1. C   2. D   3. D   4. B   5. A   6. C   7. A   8. C

BIBLE TRIVIA 2:
1. D   2. C   3. B   4. D   5. B   6. A   7. A   8. C

UNSCRAMBLE EXERCISE 1

EPTRNEEANC	REPENTANCE
DCBNOEIEE	OBEDIENCE
BISMONIUSS	SUBMISSION
FTSONMARR	TRANSFORM
OSRREET	RESTORE
RITYOVC	VICTORY
STANGIF	FASTING
CAPEE	PEACE
FOOTMCR	COMFORT
TRIMENSI	MINISTER

UNSCRAMBLE EXERCISE 2

EFEGSOVNRSI	FORGIVENESS
SRDURNERE	SURRENDER
ICTSNORINSEE	INTERCESSION
WEGRINEN	RENEWING
VOMEROCE	OVERCOME
DANCERIVEEL	DELIVERANCE
GELNOWLID	WELLDOING
PEELRH	HELPER
SCENERI	SINCERE
HEAPCR	PREACH

MATCHING EXERCISE 1

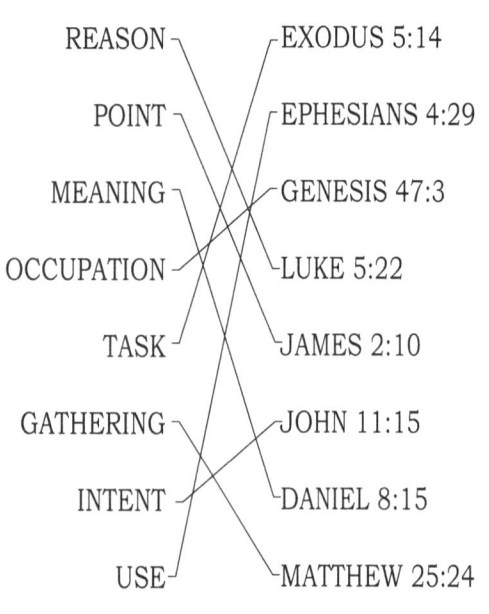

REASON — EXODUS 5:14
POINT — EPHESIANS 4:29
MEANING — GENESIS 47:3
OCCUPATION — LUKE 5:22
TASK — JAMES 2:10
GATHERING — JOHN 11:15
INTENT — DANIEL 8:15
USE — MATTHEW 25:24

MATCHING EXERCISE 2

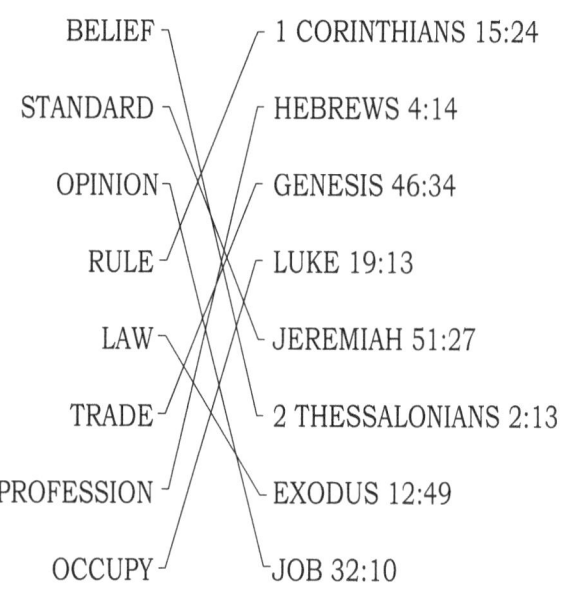

BELIEF — 1 CORINTHIANS 15:24
STANDARD — HEBREWS 4:14
OPINION — GENESIS 46:34
RULE — LUKE 19:13
LAW — JEREMIAH 51:27
TRADE — 2 THESSALONIANS 2:13
PROFESSION — EXODUS 12:49
OCCUPY — JOB 32:10

CROSSWORD 1

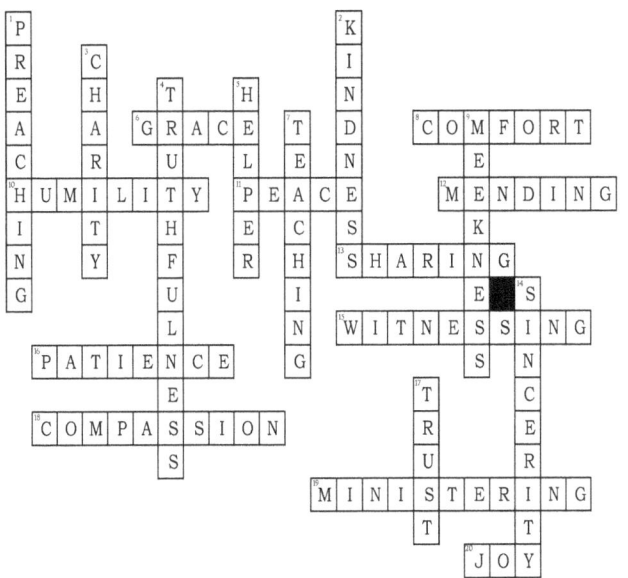

CROSSWORD 2

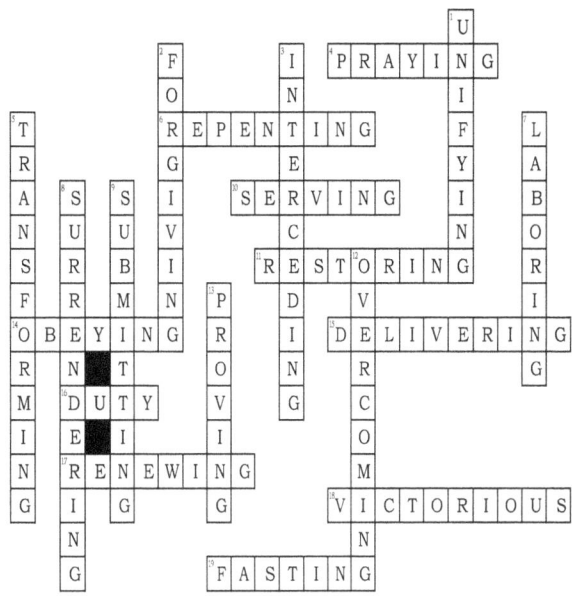

WORD SEARCH 1

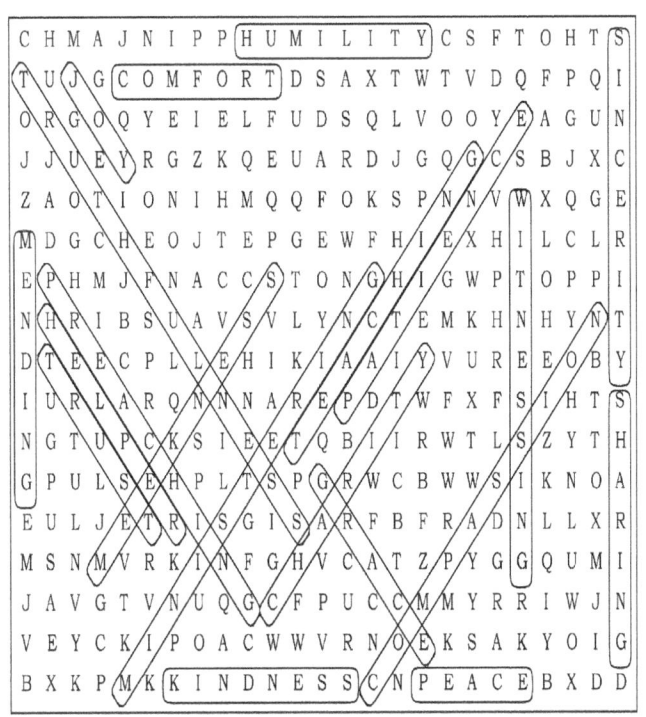

WORD SEARCH 2

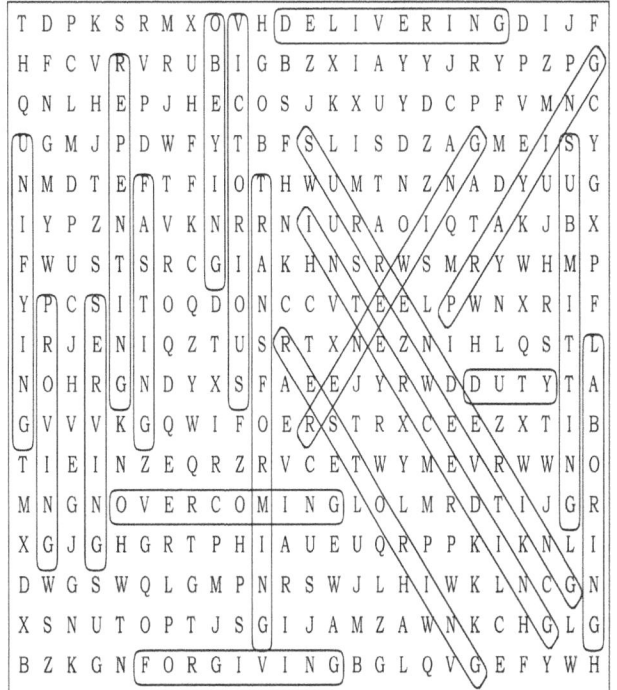

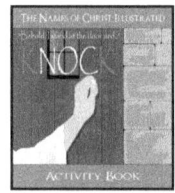 THE NOC ILLUSTRATED
ACTIVITY BOOK

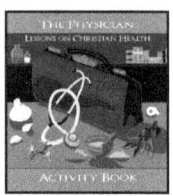 THE PHYSICIAN:
CHRISTIAN HEALTH

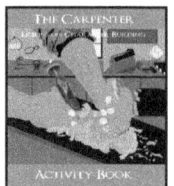 THE CARPENTER:
CHARACTER BUILDING

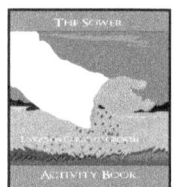 THE SOWER:
CHRISTIAN GROWTH

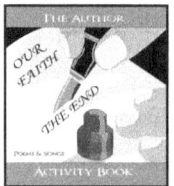 THE AUTHOR:
POEMS & SONGS

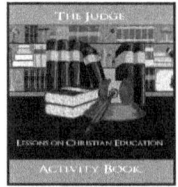 THE JUDGE:
CHRISTIAN EDUCATION

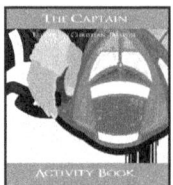 THE CAPTAIN:
CHRISTIAN PURPOSE

"PORTRAITS OF THE SAVIOUR'S
DESIRE TO ENTER HEARTS."

THIS BOOK:

THE CAPTAIN

LESSONS ON CHRISTIAN PURPOSE

THE NAMES OF CHRIST ILLUSTRATED

PLEASE VISIT US ONLINE TO VIEW
MORE GREAT TITLES AT:

WWW.THENOCILLUSTRATED.COM

www.ingramcontent.com/pod-product-compliance
Lightning Source LLC
Chambersburg PA
CBHW081239170526
45165CB00009B/3113